What happens when you give a

complete moron a crayon,

some paper, and the misguided

belief that his ignorance is worth

sharing with humankind?

You get…

LETTERS FROM T.RUMP

A Parody Book

About a Joke of a Human Being

LETTERS FROM T.RUMP

By

Dollhands T. Rump

COPYRIGHT 2023

Other Books by

Dollhands T. Rump

Our Gurney Together

How one idiot almost

killed an entire nation

during a pandemic

A Note from the Publisher

In an attempt to milk more money out of his idiot cult, the orange-colored man, who lost his bid at re-election by the widest margin in history, approached us and asked if we would print letters he had written over the years. At first, we politely declined because, honestly, who wants to waste one more minute reading the incoherent ramblings of an egotistical, shit bag of a human being? But as we were going through the piles of letters he sent to us, we couldn't help but be fascinated at the idiotic things he said to people, like President Obama and Yo-Yo Ma, or places, like KFC or a bodega on the Lower East Side, or even a few that were written to inanimate objects, (the dufus wrote letters to an actual sidewalk and a hot dog he had found and eaten), appalled, we decided to go forward with the book.

Publishing this nonsense is not meant to further his time in the spotlight. We are praying this will be his final farewell to the country he hates, his swan song if you will, before he is taken down to the shitty golf course of the underworld, where he can play the back nine with Satan, Rush Limbaugh and whoever invented black licorice. We've also arranged that all proceeds that would typically go to him, instead, will go directly to support programs that provide Drag Queens the assistance they need to continue reading to young children nationwide. This was accomplished due to his legal counsel consisting of a greasy napkin, a monkey, and Rudy Giuliani - none of which can read a contract.

We hope you enjoy the childish ramblings of a madman. We suggest reading it in his voice. Pucker your lips like a butthole, that might help. We also left in a lot of his writing mistakes, at some point, you just can't fix stupid.

This may be worth some money once he goes to prison.

Probably not.

Feel free to ban this book.

-The Publishers

LETTERS FROM T.RUMP

The Early Years

Dear Doctor,

Congratulations on being involved in my birth. How lucky you get to tell others that you helped birth a future King, or whatever it is we call those who will someday be in charge of things. It's been a few days since we first saw one another in the unfortunate region of my mother's privates, so I needed time to process what my young eyes had to witness. Perhaps a warning would have been appropriate? Anyway, concerning the events of that day, my father will be having a non-disclosure agreement sent to your office that we will need signed and notarized, not only to protect what you may have seen concerning my mother's 'trocken Wuste,' as my father calls it but also my nakedness and anything else that may have occurred during those tense and strenuous moments.

I appreciate your discretion in the matter. And again, I thank you for your professionalism in the entire affair. I had heard, while in the womb, that the best Doctors are Jews, and you lived up to that in every way by displaying an excellent bedside manner and not acting all *Jewy* in a way that makes the rest of us uncomfortable. A class act! Congratulations on witnessing the birth of what some are calling, (*their words, not mine*), the most important birth since Christ himself.

A Beautiful Baby,

Dollhands T. Rump

Dear The Colonel,

When our maid wasn't looking, I stole a piece of your chicken off my father's plate. Let me say, good sir, I think you are on to something.

The crispiness, the greasiness, and the use of a bucket as a carrying vessel. Genius!

The problem is, as a child, I am not allowed to eat things like fried chicken yet. So, I am willing to make you this proposal.

If you can have your chicken science geniuses create a baby food version of your fried chicken in what I can only assume are amazing and high-tech labs, you would bring so much joy to all the children of the world, probably to some toothless people as well.

As a young boy, I have not learned all the ins and outs of contracts and forcing you to give me money for ideas, how to be racist in my business dealings, Non-Disclosure Agreements or how to threaten to not pay any of my contractors - but as you can see, I am paying attention to how my father does business. I will someday be as great as him. Consider yourself lucky... and feel free to use my idea for free.

Oh, and not only could you make Fried Chicken Baby Food, but you could put it in tiny buckets...how great is that?

I also would like you to think about adding something to your menu that could help break the stigma of fried chicken being something mainly enjoyed by Black People. It's just not true! I love it!

Maybe something like a bucket of **ALL WHITE MEAT**, or better yet, how about you make something called Pure Fried Chicken, and instead of a bucket, invent something called a cracker barrel, just a subtle nod to the rest of us that it's a delicacy for *real* Americans as well.

Again, as a toddler, I can't use my influence to force you to pay me for any of these ideas, but if you feel obliged to thank me for the fantastic ideas I've just given you, no one is stopping you from sending me free things.

On a personal note, first, thank you for your service. I'm sure being a Colonel and running a chicken dynasty can't be easy. I would also like to compliment you on your attire; the white suit and bow tie are a wonderfully fashionable way to remind folks of the good old days when we had plantations, the Southern man was in power, and everyone knew their place.

Happy Frying!

Dollhands T. Rump

ADOLESCENCE

Dear Coach,

I am writing to ask you to please excuse Dollands from gym class for the rest of the year. He suffers from awful bone spurs that our family doctor has agreed are nearly debilitating the boy, though he looks magnificent and runs and around plays, and enjoys most sports. These bone spurs should not keep him from doing anything he wants to do, but for things like having to climb ropes, wrestle with other boys, play dodge ball or be drafted to fight in future wars, this medical ailment will most definitely be an issue. Our family doctor is also in the process of seeing if this horrible deformity could be the cause of some of his other issues, like an inability to pass both Math and English classes. Luckily this tragic medical condition, which has been bestowed upon one of the most handsome young boys of all time, has not stopped him from being able to spend hours instructing our Mexican maid how to clean the house or the Mexican gardeners how to care for the lawn, or the Mexican driver how to drive better – all while learning to read his favorite book, *Mein Kampf*, from his German Tutor, Helga. He soldiers on the way we all come to expect from such a perfect young man.

Thank you for understanding.

~~My mommy~~

His mother

Dear Pop-Tart People,

I'm a little boy who loves your tarts. I would, however, like to ask that instead of just filling them with delicious fruit flavors, how about some other flavors like popcorn, ketchup, or even, my best invention yet, a toothpaste pop tart, that way I wouldn't have to waste time brushing my teeth in the morning. I hate brushing my teeth. Your Pop-Tart could do the job for me! Genius!

If you decide to use any of my ideas, I don't need all of them named after me, maybe just a few, but I expect to be paid with money and lots of free Pop-Tarts.

I've enclosed the best address to send all the money you're going to pay me, and it is also the best place to send all the boxes of free Pop-Tarts. I am so proud to be able to help your/our company this way, as you are one of the greatest food makers of all time.

Oh, and one more last-minute idea...what if you did some science thing where instead of the white Pop-Tart turning brown when you toast it, you have it just turn whiter? I mean, seriously, who doesn't want things whiter in America? Think about it.

Oh, and if I find out that you used any of my ideas — the popcorn, the ketchup, the toothpaste, or even the whitening one, without paying me — I will have my daddy sue the shit out of your company. Then I'll own it and change the name to Rump-Tarts. And we all know Rump-Tarts would be the most incredible thing invented in the history of Earth. Keep that in mind.

Your biggest fan,

Dollhands T. Rump

Dear Lunch Ladies,

First, you're doing a bang-up job. Those square pizza slices are the best. I do, however, have a suggestion concerning the hamburgers.

We all appreciate the slightly stale bread. It's the best way to soak up the mounds of ketchup a burger deserves to be covered with. The tater tots are also a nice touch.

My issue is with the meat. Hamburger meat that is anything but crispy black is just eating raw meat. When I bite into a burger, I want the mouth feel you get when you know something has died. Any pink in the meat, you may as well ask us to walk out to a ranch and bite a cow.

I'll be so rich that I'll have my own steak company someday. I'll probably name it after myself. And people across the land will burn them until they're black, cover them with ketchup, and then brag about how rich they are.

Let's work together to make these hamburgers more like my excellent steaks of the future—just twenty or thirty more minutes on the grill. At least long enough for them to stop mooing...haha...no, but seriously, cook the damn meat.

Respectfully,

Dollhands T. Rump

Dear Boy Scout Troop 493,

With this letter, I officially resign from the Boy Scouts. After what happened during last week's camping trip, I cannot remain a part of such a sad and pitiful organization.

The weekend started great. I napped and ate snacks while you idiots learned to build tents, start fires, and tried not to pee on your beds. The only annoying part was when that bear wandered into our camp and attacked some of you. I get it, bears are scary, but the crying was a little over the top. It was just some arms and legs. There's a reason you have two of each. Calm down. They'll probably grow back. That's how science works.

That's not why I'm leaving, though. I'm going because when some genius chose to drug the adults, and that same badass stole the bus, driving you morons to the nearby town to visit the strip club, somehow that was utterly ruined as well.

You were told over and over - they like being groped. That's why they're there, but make sure you give them a few bucks before you start squeezing. How do none of you know this? Didn't your dads teach you anything?

I've heard rumors the police have been asking questions, not about the strip club, but about the hobo that somehow got run over that same night, near our camp, by what appears to have been a bus.

Coincidence!

How do you ever expect to become successful if a little thing like a hobo dying makes you act like little bitches?

When they ask you questions, you say you don't remember. It's not rocket science.

My family lawyer will also contact you to have you sign some papers and remind you I wasn't there.

Good Luck, Suckers,

Dollhands T. Rump

The Teen Years

Dear Future Me,

My writing class is making me write this stupid letter to you. Don't judge me. I know future me will think it's as lame as present me does.

I'm supposed to say things about what we 'think' the future us, meaning you, would have become.

Well, I know you don't have time to read this letter. You're probably busy making important world decisions, choosing which wife you want to kiss, or deciding whether or not to have one of your enemies or business partners executed.

Maybe all three if it's a good day!

I'm sure future me is still built like an athlete, with perfect skin, beautiful hair, and a personality that appeals to the most brilliant people in the world. I've always appealed to intelligent people. The smartest people. True story.

I'm also positive that I have either been named Mayor of New York or the King of some great country, or they've finally gotten us into space, and I'm The Ruler of Space.

Maybe I'll invent the robots. I'll train them to beat up my enemies, complain less than human women, and make me apple pies. Then again, with how these idiots run things, robots probably won't be invented until I do it as you at your current age.

Robot inventing Ruler of the Universe. Sounds amazing!

I also hope the future me created all the amazing television shows I have in mind. I thought a show where Black people and White people compete for prizes would be fun. I also had an idea where we take people we hate and send them to third-world foreign countries, strip them naked, then watch them try to find their way back home.

I also have an idea for a restaurant where we only serve animals that are so cute and adorable, they make you want to puke and deserve to be eaten—things like baby penguins and newborn elephants. We can call it Rump's Neat Eats.

You're welcome for all the great ideas I had that I'm sure you made super successful.

Well, not much else to say to future me. Congratulations on being me. Oh, and sorry about this stupid letter, but you should keep it, it will be worth lots of money someday.

Younger, Awesome You,

Dollhands T. Rump

Dear *New York Times* Movie Reviewer,

I just watched *Lord of the Flies*, a movie you highly recommended, and you now owe me money.

What a piece of trash.

It started neatly. A plane crashed, adults died, and many kids got stranded on an island. It got a little lame when the one kid wanted to create a world of communism, with everyone working together and voting on what was best for the group. How lame is that? It got good again when the cool kid said *"screw that!"*...and started a society built on the fastest and most badass in the group, created a bunch of weapons, and taught them how to hunt and act like real warriors. That was nice.

I especially like how they made fun of that fat kid. We should always take the time to make fun of fat people, short people, or anyone who is too different from us – that will help them to do better and not stand out so much and annoy the rest of us with their presence.

The leader of the cool kids was my hero. Always being angry and stealing the fat kid's glasses, then killing that pig and putting his head on a stick. Things a natural leader would do.

Unfortunately, right when the movie got to the best part, where the cool kids were going to burn the island down to catch the idiot kid and stop communism...it was **RUINED** by the adults showing up.

It does give me hope, though. It showed me that when you get a group of morons together and show them who the alpha male is (me), those idiots will do anything you say. You could be cruel and evil as long as you make them feel like someone out there wants to take away their freedoms, and they'll follow you anywhere. That's good to know.

So really, what your review should have said was, it's an excellent movie, as the remarkable and influential people were finally allowed to run things the way they knew was best, but got ruined when the communist kid was suddenly given a handout by the adults, who always ruin everything.

So, you owe me the price of a ticket. You also owe me what I spent on snacks

— one large popcorn, one bag of peanuts, two chocolate bars, one box of licorice, and seven Diet Cokes.

I'd also like a printed apology in your paper. My dad's lawyers will be contacting your lawyers.

Love of Non-Commmie Movies,

Dollhands T. Rump

Dear **NASA**,

I have a question for you. I will someday be your most famous astronaut, the best, and I'll discover all the planets and date all the sexy aliens, just like that guy on Star Trek.

I've been told being an astronaut isn't easy. Lots of school and training and stuff, none of which interests me, so I came up with a better idea.

I've noticed you all are big on the Tang. Everyone at **NASA** is drinking Tang. You even do commercials for it. Tang Tang Tang!

So I had my dad hire some scientists. The smartest scientists. They took some Tang and did some experiments on it, and they said they thought my theory was correct — Tang creates astronauts!

I figured out your secret.

All those things about joining the military, flying jets, and being super bright were all just a cover-up to make people think being able to fly to the moon was only for a few chosen people.

I won't tell your secret to anyone.

So, as of a month ago, I've been drinking as much Tang as possible. I'm up to 6 gallons a day! When I reach an appropriate astronaut age, I will reach out to you, and we can create magic together. I'll even pretend to be in the military and fly in jets. You can get pictures of me wearing uniforms and saluting and stuff because I understand how good **PR** works.

I do have one question, though.

The real reason I'm writing you is because I was wondering if you've noticed any side effects with your astronauts as far as the Tang is involved? I'm just spit-balling here, but maybe things like elevated blood sugar levels, increased weight gain, a large amount of cavities, and skin pigment turning more of an orange hue than is considered normal?

Not that any of these have happened to me, but I want to make sure I've covered all my bases, as any intelligent person would do.

So please let me know if any of these things I've never had an issue with yet, especially the orange skin, is something I should be concerned about.

Meanwhile, I'll keep up with my 'training,' and you now have a heads-up preparing **NASA** for what will be an exciting new adventure, Rump in Space!

And don't worry, I'll keep your secret a secret. I'm good at keeping secrets. I never told anyone about when you tried to fake that moon landing back in the day. That was so silly, but I understood it was to make America look great and to be first, and we all know nothing is too far or too illegal to make sure we're number one!

Happy Flying!

Dollhands T. Rump (future astronaut)

Dear English Teacher,

I noticed on our last essay you got a little stir krazy with your red pen. Whenever I substituted the letter **C** with the letter **K**, you akted like a horrible krime had been kommitted. You and I both know that not only does it make sense to use a **K** when the sound is a **K** sound, but it's also more pleasing to the eye, as the letter **C** looks sad and mopey, and the **K** looks big and strong and ready to kikk ass. Did you notice the word 'kick' has typically **TWO K**'s and only one **C**? But when I made it like **KiKK** ass, it was so much kooler because three **K**s, for some reason, always look purer, somehow. It must be a science thing.

Anyway, I will give you one more chance to grade the paper korrektly, now that you understand that I'm koming from a place of science. If it sounds like a **K**, then it shouldn't be a **C**, because if we aren't going to be unique and kikk ass when we need to be, what type of kountry will we bekome?

I appreciate your taking the time to look this over, and no worries, I won't have my parents komplain to the skhool board about this unless you and I kannot kome to an agreement.

Respektfully Yours,

Dollhands T. Rump

Dear Father Joseph,

Let me begin by saying how pleased I was to hear you are back home from your brief hospital stay.

Secondly, let me apologize to you. I honestly have no recollection of that evening.

In my defense, I still don't understand why a priest was called at all. Nothing inappropriate or demonic was going on in my bedroom that night.

I read the police report that said my skin had an *unnatural* orange appearance. It's an astronaut thing — you wouldn't understand. It also said my hair had an other-worldly, straw-like look to it. I have luscious locks. Blame God.

Most offensive were the things you wrote down as **Signs Demonic Possession: S**pitting, cussing, yelling, peeing myself, making my mouth look like a butthole, racial slurs, misogynistic rants, nazi salutes, and a detailed subscription of me trying to grab our maid. Lies! Plus, she likes it. All women do.

Anyway, I'm sorry you got hurt, but look at the bright side, it's not like I bruised anything you get to use as a priest anyway, right?

I hope not, anyway.

I've heard rumors.

Blessings Padre,

Dollhands T. Rump

Young Adult Years

R

Dear President Nixon,

I wanted to be you when I grew up. I say *wanted* because I lost much respect for you this week.

Why did you cave? They had some recordings of you saying some things. Who cares? You're the President! You have immunity for everything you do. You could kill a bus of orphans, and they can't touch you. Well, that and all the free hookers and cocaine, I'm sure that's great too! That's the best gift about being President.

I think you should have called their bluff and just nuked them. All of them. The investigators, the Democrats, and anyone who didn't bow to your greatness. A bomb up the ass, and you can write on each one *Love Dick!* That would be great!

Who am I kidding? I can't be mad at you. I love you. You are the greatest thing to happen to America since the McCarthy Hearings. I read about those in school, and I can't wait until America is great like that again!

President Nixon, sir, I make you this promise – someday I will become President or King or whatever, and I will make sure I continue what you started, making America look more like the country we know it can be instead of what the communists and illegals are doing to it.

I'll make sure your head is carved in Mt. Rushmore next to mine, and I'll have statues of you at every one of the many buildings I will own. We'll make sure New York City is covered with bronze Dicks.

I promise to write you if you go to prison. Ha-ha, I'm kidding. Everyone knows rich and powerful men don't go to jail. (wink)

Keep your head up. Real Americans know all the great things you did for our country. History will show that you were a genius.

I love you,

Dollhands T. Rump

Dear Army Draft Board,

Thank you for understanding that due to my horrible bone spurs, I cannot fight alongside my American brothers against our enemies, be they brown, black, or other shades of brown.

It breaks my heart not to be able to wave the American flag while standing over the bodies of all the horrible enemies that hate our freedom.

After playing football, rugby, tennis, track, and a brief time playing volleyball, our family doctor was shocked to discover that my bone spurs would cause me to be more of a hindrance than a help in the campaign towards spreading Americanism around the world.

As I sit at home, I will never forget those who are out there eating out of cans, sleeping in the mud, and having bits of themselves shot off by stray bullets — and every time I golf 18 holes or sit down to a beautiful meal of burnt steak or chicken out of a bucket, I will eat it with a bit of guilt, knowing my brothers-in-arms don't have it so good. I'll also eat it with ketchup, but definitely guilt too.

If, by some miracle, my bone spurs heal enough so that I can put on a green uniform and head out to help you all kill the brown people, you can bet I will be there. I will be the best soldier you've ever had. I've had many people who serve, many of them, say to me, 'Dollhands, we can tell by just looking at you, you would be the best soldier probably in the history of this country.' It's true.

I also promise that if I ever run for public office, like Mayor, President, or King, I will never disparage or attack anyone who has served our county with honor—especially **POWs**. We should always respect them; only a traitor to America would attack a **POW**.

God's **S**peed,

Dollhands **T. R**ump

Dear *New York Times* Movie Reviewer,

Again, you screwed up.

How the hell did you think *9 to 5* was a good movie?

Maybe you're some sort of weirdo, commie, pinko feminist...to quote the great Archie Bunker.

It's a movie showing women having **NO** respect for their boss. A successful White man, just trying to keep his company profitable, being nice to his lady-helpers by complimenting them about how hot they look, and they treat him so horribly!

It wasn't a comedy at all! It was a horror movie for successful businessmen like me. Dabney Coleman deserves an Oscar for keeping it together as long as he did. Maybe we can give a couple of tiny Oscars to Dolly Parton's boobs, because who doesn't love those...but aside from that, it was an awful movie about women not respecting men, men being blamed for things that used to be what made this country great, and shows why giving jobs to unattractive women will always backfire in America.

Shame on you for telling anyone to see this piece of trash. I can only assume your father was unsuccessful in business, and your mother was secretly a lesbian. You should remove that typewriter from your office and put in a punching bag; that way, you can remember what being a man is supposed to feel like.

You should lay off the fancy coffee drinks too. All the drizzles and whipped creams may be bringing down your testosterone levels.

I'm sending you a picture of Dolly Parton's boobs as well. The fact that you didn't mention them at all in your review shows just how far you've fallen from the Man Wagon. I expect an apology letter to be printed immediately!

Grrrrrr...

Dollhands T. Rump

Man Baby Years

Dear Nuns,

I was walking down Fifth Avenue the other day and ran into a group of you. Are you called a group? Is it a cackle? A cackle of Nuns? A herd? Herd of Nuns... that sounds good. Anyway, I ran into a herd of you, and I have to say, those are some damn unattractive outfits you wore. What is that, wool? I swear, even when I squinted, I couldn't even see any ankle. How the hell do you expect to get a good man when you're pretty much dressed in wool sacks?

I also think walking around in a gang isn't helping, either. It's almost like you're trying to keep the men away. Are you lesbians? It's okay if you are. I love lesbians. Some of my favorite movies have lesbians in them.

Anyway, take it from me, someone who plans on having a lot of wives, even I would have a hard time getting aroused around a herd of wool-wearing ladies who look like they are headed to an Indigo Girls concert.

Don't you have the internet? Nun outfits can be super sexy if you pick the right ones. They don't always have to be fake leather, but it doesn't hurt!

If you go to the google and type in Sexy Nun Outfit, you'll have more than enough choices to make yourselves look like something a real man would like. I'm sure there are guys out there into girls who are all into the church stuff, but not me. I want my wives to be godless and without morals, the way God intended.

I'll also write a letter to your boss, that pope guy, and tell him about the sexy nun outfits online. Heck, that guy wears prettier dresses than you... let's talk about that, right?

Remember, if God made you hot, it's a sin to hide it. If you made you not so hot, feel free to cover up, no one wants to see that.

God love ya,

Dollhands T. Rump

Dear Pope,

I just wrote a letter to a group of nuns I saw walking around the city looking like homeless kids from a sad, art film about homeless kids.

You can't honestly tell me that with all the millions of dollars the Vatican has, all the jewels and fancy dresses you wear all day, no one thinks helping these women look like women would be a bad idea? And why punish the men who go to church?

As I told the ladies, just google Sexy Nun Outfit. You're welcome.

If you ever come to New York, look me up. We'll put some man clothes on you, I'll take you to all the fanciest places, and maybe we'll even find you a wife. It doesn't look good, a man of your wealth and power without a dame on his arm. People will talk.

Sincerely,

Dollhands T. Rump

Dear Department Stores of America,

Serious question...why do you make ties so damn short? It's almost like you used midgets as models. Oh, I'm sorry, we're not supposed to call them midgets anymore. What are they now? Small humans? Baby Adults? Shorties? I like Baby Adults. I'll use that.

Anyway, what the hell is the point of making a tie that doesn't even cover your amazing abs? Let me tell you, I have some amazing abs. It's true. People who work out every day come up to me, and they're like, "Mr. Rump, how do you do it? We work out all day and can't get amazing abs like you!" I'm serious. And I tell them the truth. It's all-natural. I haven't worked out a day in my life. When I was young, I played sports and stuff, just like every other kid with bone spurs, but once I became an adult, I just looked at my gut and said **STRAIGHTEN UP!**...and it worked. Abs like Adonis. The most amazing abs. Everyone says so.

Anyway, not having a tie that goes past the abs, over the belt buckle, and then over the penis area...how is that not a thing? If you look at me from behind and can't see my tie dangling between my legs, like the balls of a **Pit Bull** that hasn't been fixed, what's the point of even wearing a tie? It's a power statement! The longer the tie, the larger the bank account. That's why I have the most enormous ties. And why my bank account is **HUGE!**

Anyway, I will need you all to go ahead and fire all those Baby Adults, hire some normal-size people, preferably with great abs like me, and make some goddamn ties that show the world how successful you are. I also have some thoughts about suits, but for now, focus on those ties. I'm tired of paying my guy extra to put together two ties to make one normal one. **THAT'S A WASTE OF MONEY!**

You're Welcome,

Dollands T. Rump

Dear Street Hot Dog,

I want to apologize. I've always been told, by my flunkies, that street hot dogs are the best. I couldn't imagine that being true. Some of them would go on and on about the skin snap, the bun's warmth, and the red sauce's tang. They often say the one's around Central Park are the best. That always sounded vile to me.

I stand corrected. I was walking down 3rd Avenue yesterday after a meeting with a contractor I refused to pay because of shoddy work, and I stumbled upon one on the street.

There it was, in all its glory, a hot dog with red sauce on top of half a napkin. I bent over and picked it up off the ground. It had a few ants on it, but I flicked those bastards off. It was still warm.

It could have used more ketchup, like everything in life, but it was still enjoyable. When I bit it, I could feel and hear the pop of the weenie skin that others had bragged about. I was in heaven.

I only have two complaints. It seems odd to have them lying around in the streets like that, and walking around and staring at the ground when hungry sounds annoying. Perhaps you should have a cart where people can step up and order one. I also couldn't figure out who to pay. If you don't make money from something, what's even the point of doing it? Bad business model.

My recommendations are a centralized location, or better yet, you could have many locations around the city. Imagine that! And you definitely need to charge people money, maybe extra on weekends, when all the idiot tourists are here. Finally, and most importantly, more ketchup. Like I always say, 'If it ain't covered in ketchup, it ain't real food.'

I considered making this my new business venture. But my accountants told me it would not be in my interest at this time, as we're currently in the middle of various lawsuits for racism, not paying contractors and multiple charges of rape. After the success of **Rump Steaks, Rump Vodka, and Rump Real Estate**...who wouldn't want to bite into a **Rump Weenie**, right?

They were also a little concerned that calling something a **Rump Weenie** might hurt my chances of being President someday since we all know a large part of my base will consist of homophobic Americans. **Not** that a lot of them won't secretly enjoy a **Rump Weenie** in the privacy of their own homes, since most homophobes are actually just conservative, gay men confused with their own inner-thoughts and urges (I'm looking at you, **Senator**), but still, why take the chance? Maybe next year!

A New Fan,

Dollhands T. Rump

Dear *Vogue Magazine*,

I've heard you wanted to do an article about the most fashionable men in New York City. I had a better idea. Why waste time talking to all the other buffoons on the island when you can devote the magazine to me.

I'm aware of how amazing I am. Tailor-made suits, custom-made ties, and shoes made of the finest skin from the most endangered animals on Earth.

And though they say the suit makes the man, which it does, it turns out the man also makes the man. I'm even amazing naked!

At my golf club, in the locker room, I've had the most impressive male models, handsome young men, approach me and ask me how I keep in such fantastic shape. I tell them the truth — genetics. My **DNA** is sexy. And no, having handsome men approach me in the locker room doesn't make me gay, it makes me a stud.

I also get many compliments about my hair. My golden locks, as I call them. The style is something no one has ever been able to replicate, and for a good reason, it's been a secret for almost my entire life.

I will allow you to print my hair secret if you devote the entire magazine to me. You'll find it fascinating.

Two words. Carnival King.

What's Carnival King? Let me start from the beginning. As a young boy in my early twenties, I enjoyed life like most young boys—sports, girls, daddy's money, etc. I was a handsome lad, clean-cut and sexy. Everyone said so. I honestly didn't think any part of me could improve. Boy, was I wrong!

I was at the New Jersey State Fair with a beautiful girl, I can't remember her name, but I do remember she had a great rack and smelled like jelly beans.

We were walking through the food area when we heard a commotion. A horse had broken free from the rodeo area and ran wild, trampling kids and adults. My date, the one with the boobs, took matters into her own hands and pushed me out of the way of the deadly beast.

I flew about ten feet and landed in the Carnival King. What could that have been, you ask? Simple. Carnival King is a cotton candy machine. One of those big metal tubs where you swirl the paper cones around, and it magically creates cotton candy. I'm not sure how they work, I still don't know, but I'm pretty sure it's witchcraft.

So, there I am, one minute about to be killed by a giant horse, and the next minute I'm head first in a Carnival King. The crowd is screaming, the horse is trampling, and this machine is just whirring and whirring around my head, which had become lodged in the center of it.

Once the man turned the machine off and they pulled me out, the crowd gasped. A real gasp. It was full of awe and amazement. That machine created this beautiful coif of hair I'm known for worldwide. World leaders have called it stunning. Models and porn stars have begged me to let them touch it. Some men even said an hour with my hair makes them question their sexuality.

I even went out and bought my own Carnival King. I keep one in every home I own, and every morning, after my morning delousing, I stick my beautiful head in it and come out the majestic, golden hair I'm famous for.

I have so many more stories that your readers will love. How I get my ties so long and beautiful. Why my suits look too big but aren't. An exciting account about my amazing tan, which involves NASA, the moon and gallons of Tang. All yours, but only if you want to sell the most magazines in the history of all magazines. It's up to you.

When I tell that story about my hair, people always ask me what happened to the big-boobed girl that pushed me out of the way of that crazy horse. I think I heard she was trampled to death, poor thing, she never got to see my amazing new hair!

The Carnival King,

Dollhands T. Rump

Dear Mrs. America Pageant,

I've decided I'm going to take over your franchise. I've loved your show for years, but to be honest, the last few years have been lackluster at best.

Can you believe a show that promotes hot women can be lackluster? Me neither!

So, here's my plan. First, we're going to fire everyone. We're starting the whole thing over. Second, along with the Mrs. America, I would also like to take over Ms. America and Miss Teen America. Hot married women are great. Who doesn't want to fantasize about another man's wife? But women who haven't been married are also hot, and young ladies who are soon-to-be women are hot too.

I remember watching my daughter grow from a cute teen into a sexy young lady and now a beautiful woman. I got to see it all. I've said it many times, out loud, even on video; I would have married her if that was legal. I know it's not. Calm down.

After we fire everyone, we will rework how the pageant is done. First, we will remove boring stuff like evening gowns and questions about world events. No one cares what you think about an earthquake halfway around the world or how you wish we would feed starving kids or find homes for cats, leave that to the ugly girls. And we don't care what you'd wear to a fancy restaurant. People want to be entertained with fantasy and what-ifs.

We'll keep the swimsuit part of it, but only bikinis or less will be allowed, preferably less. We'll also keep the talent portion, but we're going to mix in cool costumes. They will dress as something sexy, like a sexy nurse, a sexy cheerleader or a sexy waitress — their choice — then they do their talent. They need to make it believable!

We may also add a sexy nighttime outfit portion, or maybe something where they wear a skin-tight one-piece like those fancy French ladies wear in *Cirque de Soleil.* They could roll around in something like Jello or various oils. I don't know. Just spit-balling ideas here.

I also have a ton of ideas for the Miss Teen Pageant. Sadly, my dumb lawyers haven't been able to find ways to do any of them, at least without breaking a lot of laws in every State — dumb legal system. We'll keep you updated.

The other new things are - I'm the only judge, and before the pageant, I get to spend at least an hour which each contestant, getting to know them better. And if I can't decide between two of the girls, we may have them do something like a sing-off, juggling, or maybe a no-holds-barred fight in a cage.

We'll have the highest-rated shows in the history of television. And really, there are no losers. Even the girl who comes in last will be beautiful...and we all know beautiful people are guaranteed extraordinary lives.

The New Owner of Sexy American Wives, Single Ladies and Teens,

Dollhands T. Rump

Dear All Ivy League Colleges,

First, let me start by saying I have no respect for your Liberal-focused machines of Socialism that churn out a bunch of nepo-babies who couldn't survive on their own, in the real world, without daddy's money. Sure, I accepted a buck or two from my father to appease the old man, but then I went out and made my fortune on my own.

But that's not why I'm writing you.

I'm writing you because when I decided to get a college diploma (not because I needed one, it's just a stupid piece of paper, but I thought it would be fun to hang on my wall next to my covers of *Time Magazine* that have my face on them, an autographed photo of Linda Ronstadt a friend sold to me who was also named Dollhands, and a one-of-a-kind reproduction of a letter written by the great General Robert E. Lee, just before the Socialists cheated and won the war). I could show it to all my friends, and we could have a good laugh that someone of my stature would attend a shithole institution like yours.

Anyway, it turned out that you were all so threatened by my genius and the attention I would take away from you, and all your donations would probably start coming to me, so you refused me entry. That's fine. I went to the world-renowned Wharton School of Business, where I become the best student they've ever had, true story, I was so bright some of the teachers would sit down and ask me to teach the classes...but I was like, 'No, you get up there and earn your paycheck, I'll just let you know when you are wrong'…and they were like, 'wow, thank you!' Truth!

So now that I've graduated and have taken over my father's booming real estate business, to make it even more successful, I've decided I'm going to open my own University. But not a little bitch college like yours, full of Communists and Marxists. This beautiful place will teach how to make money, how to make more money, and then when you think all the money has been made, how to get people to send you their money, so you can use it to make more money. I'm also going to call it Rump College. It's going to be amazing. And you'll all BEG me to join your Ivy League, but I'll shake my head and say no, sorry, I don't join commie clubs.

Rump University. It's going to be amazing. I am still deciding on a mascot. I've narrowed it down to an Eagle, a Wolverine, or a Big Hand that I can bitch-slap you all with. Ha! Suck it!

Best Graduate of Wharton School of Business,

Dollands T. Rump

Dear Bodega Down the Street from Rump Tower,

Ola. I assume you speak Spanish. It's hard for me to figure out what type of brown you are, but I don't know how Indians or Haitians say hello, so we'll stick to Ola!

I accidentally walked into your place of business a few months ago. Someone I owed money was coming down the street, and I needed a place to duck away for a moment, not because I was afraid of them, but because I was wearing my favorite tie and I didn't want to get blood on it if I had to kick their ass.

Anyway, the few seconds I spent in your shack, or Palace as you probably call it, as I'm sure you've never had anything that nice back in whatever shithole country you're from, I had an idea. Besides the magazines, sodas, and random piles of fruit, The stacks of energy drinks, cigarettes, and lottery ticket machine. The condoms, the Twinkies, and something that looked like a boiled egg on a plate wrapped in plastic...I noticed you didn't offer anything of value, like steaks.

So here how that day will become magical for you. You, a poor immigrant from a shithole country, just scraping by offering random shit to lost tourists...and myself, one of the most famous and rich men in all the world, stepping into your store, a moment that you will now see is about to change your whole life.

Two words. **Rump Steaks.**

That's right! I have a line of steaks. They're the best steaks. Everyone says so. Each steak is carefully sliced from the dead carcass of a cow that lived an unbelievable life. You hear about those cows in Japan that drink beer, get a massage, and live an extraordinary life to make that beef that sells for lots of money? Mine are better!

My cows don't drink beer. They drink champagne. The good stuff. They don't just get massages. I make sure every massage ends with a happy ending, because we all know that a massage without a happy ending isn't even authentic – and you should ask for your money back.

My cows walk on plush rugs, thousands of rugs spread out like a giant outdoor opium den. We also give them opium, but not too much, just enough to keep them returning. We also have music playing softly in the background. American bands only.

After a lifetime of champagne, rugs, and happy endings, these cows are gently lulled into an opium-induced euphoria and led to a French Guillotine I bought my first wife for our wedding. I knew it would come in handy someday.

Then the meat is sectioned off into beautiful steaks and other meat things, packaged in wrapping that looks like it's made out of gold, and sent around the world to those who only want the best steaks. The best thing, and you'll love this, the meat is so hardy and excellent you can burn it to a crisp, exactly the way a steak should be cooked, then smother it in ketchup for your eating pleasure.

So I'll put you down for 100 steaks to start with. You'll have to make room in your refrigerator, but honestly, all that milk and yogurt you were carrying can be put on the shelf, they'll be fine.

After you get wealthy from selling my excellent steaks, you can move back to your crap country and open a store there. I know how your people always talk about making money in America so you can bring your family over here, but honestly, we're pretty full up now with your types. Plus, here, you'll only be middle class, where you're from, you'll be the wealthiest man in town! You're welcome. Expect a delivery soon, Amigo.

The Steak King,

Dollhands T. Rump

Dear Netflix,

The other night, after wife #3 had gone to her separate bedroom, I was flipping through your offerings and stumbled upon a movie called *Trading Places*.

I usually don't watch anything that doesn't have me in it, like that fantastic *Home Alone* in New York movie, which I highly recommend. Some say my appearance is what made the film so successful. In fact, they wanted to invent a category for me at the Oscars. An award for a brief appearance in a movie, but I said no, let's not take away from all those Hollywood actors who work so hard to achieve fame and fortune, so they said, okay, Mr. Rump, but if you ever change your mind, we're happy to give you the award you deserve. So kind of them.

Anyway, I decided to put on this *Trading Places* movie, and I was excited to see that it was about two wealthy and powerful men who had decided to make a bet about how they could play with the lives of some little people.

You see, I do that all the time! I love to pit my employees against each other. Sometimes I make them do things, and the prizes are one gets promoted, and the other gets fired. They love it! For a while, we even had a venue in Queens where we would all bring our best House Maids, and they would fight it out in a sort of Octagon cage thing. I used to take my maid, Margarita, there every Friday night after her shift. She wasn't as good as I had hoped in the beginning. But I made her pay for some fighting classes, and we found a steroid that her stomach could tolerate, and then she started to kick everyone's ass. There's nothing like seeing a proud Mexican woman wearing her maid outfit, covered in blood, holding her hands over her head in victory after destroying another brown lady. She loved it.

Sadly, due to some stomach complications, she is no longer with us. She's buried by the 12th hole at my golf course in Jersey. But I digress.

The movie was great because it showed how fun it is to be rich and use your power to make others perform for you. I even got to do it for a while on national television, where people did stupid shit, and then, in the end, I would fire someone. It was great fun.

Sadly, the movie ended with the poor people making fools of the rich guys, which is always how stupid movies from Hollywood end since they're all Socialists and Commies in Hollywood. So, I will stick to watching movies that star me in them. Anyway, that was the point of my letter, how about more movies starring me in them? You can call it your American Stud Series.

Did I mention the Academy wanted to give me a special Oscar for my acting? It's true. Ask anyone.

Best Actor Ever,

Dollhands T. Rump

New York Orphanage,

So let's say your wife gives birth, and he is a pretty ugly baby, and then he grows into a rather dull kid. Looking at him annoys you, and you know it's only going to get worse because he's already ten and he hasn't improved in any noticeable way. It's heartbreaking.

My question is...do you buy kids like that?

Let's also say this boring kid talks like he's got rocks in his mouth and, frankly, acts like he has rocks in his head. He can't tie his shoes, is barely potty trained, has a cow-lick like that idiot Dennis the Menace, and his teeth are obviously going to come out looking like a rabbit. Do things like that make it harder or easier to find them a home?

Let's also say he walks around like he's always confused; the kid can't tell if he's coming or going. He eats with his mouth full, and if you shout at him **DON'T EAT WITH YOUR MOUTH FULL**, he smiles at you with his little rabbit teeth but keeps chomping away like a camel.

Oh, and he only likes to eat pancakes. Just pancakes. Like some mentally-challenged kid born under the stove at a Waffle House, he insists on using that syrup with the black lady on it because he thinks it looks like one of our maids, or all of them, who knows.

I mean, seriously, there **HAS** to be an idiotic, liberal, young couple out there who likes to save stupid, homeless cats and dogs from puppy mills and thinks recycling matters and wants to save the Earth and somehow, in their hippy-dippy brains, feels helping an idiot child amount to something in the world, would be worth wasting their time on, right?

At first, I thought I would offer him to you for about a million dollars. Not because he's worth more than a buck, but because he comes from some fantastic DNA...and yes, I had him tested because honestly, for a while there, I was convinced my ex-wife had to have had sex with a bag of Styrofoam to make something this dumb, but nope, he's my kid (I must have been running a fever that day), however, after writing this all down, I'm now changing my offer. I'm willing to let him go for a thousand bucks. Or ten bucks. Or free. I don't care. I need him gone. I'm going to kill this kid, and even though I'm rich and powerful, as we've seen repeatedly, even killing your kid is somehow a crime in this country. It doesn't make sense since I made him, but whatever.

Come get him, and don't worry about me being lonely. I have the most amazing, sexy, and beautiful daughter. She's the best thing that's ever happened to me that wasn't money-related. I'd marry her myself if that wasn't illegal (believe me, I've checked). I have great plans for her. I plan on having her marry someone rich but with little-to-no personality. Maybe a little Jewish guy with pasty skin. Someone just man enough to give me grandkids but just weird enough that we will always know Daddy's her favorite.

I also have a son that I named after me. He's an idiot but smart enough to know his place. He's easy to manipulate, and I always tell him what a big man he is. That makes him happy. I'm sure he'll be in jail someday or develop a drug habit, but he's a good kid for now. Oh, and I always forget I have another daughter from another wife. I can't remember her name right now, but she's not bad looking and will probably do things in life. Who knows.

Anyway, as you can see, I'm a great father, and my other kids are proof of that. In fact, important people wanted to invent an award for me and call me the *Father of the Century*. True story.

They would have a big event, an award ceremony, and maybe even name something after me, like a building or a ship. But I was like 'no, that's okay, all fathers need to be recognized, let's keep it the way it is'. They were so impressed they wanted to give me an award because of how humble I am, but I said 'no, I don't want to boast about how humble I am'. All true.

So now that you know I'm an amazing Dad, you can understand there's no fixing stupid. I will leave word with our doorman that when you drop by, to let in. You can grab that little jerk and sell him to a loving home. Tell you what – to sweeten the deal, I will pay you a hundred thousand dollars to take him. That's almost as much as I pay porn stars. How's that for fatherly love???

He doesn't have anything you need to take with you. The kid's happy staring at a stick all day. Come and get him. Please. His name is Eric.

Best Dad Ever,

Dollhands T. Rump

Dear **QVC**,

First of all, huge fan. I love how you sell items for more than they're worth and ask people to pay in installments because that makes them feel like they're paying less. **G**enius!

It's kind of you to give semi-attractive, old models something to do. **G**ood for them still feeling pretty, and good for you still pretending they don't look like someone's mom.

Now the reason I'm writing you is because I've been tossing around an idea in my big brain - it's time you and I went into business together. We know what you have to offer. A payment plan that takes money from idiots and mediocre middle-aged models and a channel that reaches millions of Americans twenty-four hours a day.

And what do I have to offer? The answer is, well, everything!

Besides my Real Estate Empire, my Casinos, and my Golf Courses — I've also put my amazing Midas touch on things that can easily make millions for you and me. We can sell Rump Steaks, Rump Vodka, Rump Phone Chargers, Rump Kitty Litter, Rump Duck Whistles, Rump Baby Wipes, Rump Extra-long Ties, Rump Shoe Shine Kits, Rump Gold Bars, Rump Native American Bible Covers, Rump Scar Remover and Skin Softener, Rump Gun Range Targets, Rump Ketchup, and Rump Condoms....I also have a few thousand copies of my book that we can sell!

I'm excited!

Here are my terms. I'm not sure what you pay those idiots who sell air fryers and those weird lesbian-looking pants, but I expect 80% of every sale. You pay all shipping fees. I get to sell all my items myself, and you can give me a sidekick if you want, someone to act excited when I talk, but it has to be a hot chick of my choosing, no PTA-looking women, and no feminine guys with their weak wrists.

I also get to decide what time of day I get to be on tv, complete control of production, and my own hair and makeup team.

We can start small at first. I say we go with my book, the vodka, the steaks, and the condoms. Oh, I just had a great idea! We can do a gift basket with my book, a bottle of vodka, a steak, and some condoms. We'll call in the *Rump and Chill Basket*. I'm a genius! This is going to be great. My lawyers will contact you soon.

Your Future Partner,

Dollhands T. Rump

Dear Elon Musk,

First, let me say; I'm a huge fan. Anyone who can piss everyone off while making money, that's something to be admired. I like those cars you're making too. I don't drive, I want to leave that to the darker people, but I have heard those cars you make are pretty amazing. I heard a rumor that they even make fart noises. That's hilarious! My latest wife would hate that. She can't stand when I fart around the house. She's a prude, but she's hot. I'll send you her nudes later so you can see I married the most seductive woman.

Anyway, I've heard rumors that you plan on flying rich people to the Moon, space, or whatever. That's great. I wanted to plant a little idea in your head. Once you colonize the Moon, get rid of all the Illegals or whatever you find up there, and plant some stuff and make it pleasant, you'll need someone to build big, beautiful hotels for the people who want to stay up there.

Here's what I'm thinking. Some space resorts, a few golf courses, and an amusement park. It will be insane. People will be so freaked out they're on the Moon they'll buy anything. We can just put rocks in a box, call it a fucking moon rock, and they'll pay a hundred bucks for it.

Anyway, I know we're a long way from a Rump Resort on the Moon, or Rump Moontower as I call it, but when the time comes, we can have a beautiful friendship.

Oh, and between you and me, when you start building your bus rockets to go up there, you should make them look like penises as much as possible. A real penis, with a little mushroom on top, the way normal penises look. Men will feel manly looking at it, and women will love it. They love that shit. Trust me.

Talk to you in the Future!

Dollhands T. Rump

Dear Senator from North Carolina,

Stop.

Texting.

Me.

All.

The.

Fucking.

Time.

How do you even have my number?

Dollhands T. Rump

Dear New York Taxi Company,

I want to lodge a formal complaint. First of all, let me clarify that I never have, and would never, ride in a taxi. No offense. They're just shitty cars that poor people use. Gross.

I have my own car and driver, thank you very much. But as a New Yorker, who has to see the cabs every day, and a man of prestige in this city, I feel it is my place to let you know of the following:

Hiring a bunch of foreigners doesn't look good. Think about it. You have these idiot tourists from Iowa and Nebraska who come here with their overalls and buckteeth and cameras around their necks, and they want to experience the true New York, a welcoming city of money and real estate, not a smelly cab driven by a guy who doesn't even speak English.

Now don't get me wrong, I'm not a racist. In fact, I'm the least racist person in America. It's true. Many people think so. I think something as American as a New York cab ride should be as American as possible. Sure, we're a city of immigrants or are least until I become Mayor someday, then we can figure out who goes where, but until then, I'm willing to play along.

Here's my proposal. How about we hire decent, American-speaking, lighter folks to drive the cabs, and maybe we can give them uniforms, like a turban or a sombrero, to look like they belong to this or that working class, but in reality, they're a bunch of dorks from the Midwest, able to speak English and engage with the tourist. It will be like that *Small World* ride in at Disneyland, all countries represented, but really, just a bunch of little German kids in costumes. Genius.

Oh, and your cabs being yellow sucks. That's the color of hair, not vehicles. I suggest a lovely green, the color of money.

Beep Beep,

Dollhands T. Rump

Dear Mr. Putin,

I've been watching you from afar and am a huge fan. My people have been urging me toward running for President, they say I would be the best President since Abraham Lincoln, their words, not mine, and I agree with them. If I decide to run, I have a few questions since you've mastered the game so well.

How do you keep your people in line? It's a thing of beauty. I especially like how those who try to cause trouble keep accidentally throwing themselves out of windows or ingesting poison. Nice touch.

When your enemies have become too vocal, how exactly do you lure them to the higher floors of a building? And once there, do you pretend that you see something in the street below, and ask them to come and look, then give them a gentle pat on the back? Or is it something else altogether?

Also, when one of your enemies accidentally ingests poison, is it a particular type? Do you like when they fall to the ground and foam at the mouth before they die, or is it the slower type, where they feel a little off for a few days or weeks, then their body starts to wither away?

I would like the slower one because it would be fun to be around someone that kept saying they didn't feel well, and I would have to keep a straight face, knowing it wasn't just a cold they were fighting off. Any tips would help. I could do it. I'm the best actor. I want to be for America what you are for Russia.

I'm also a big fan of your parades. Big missiles going down the street. That's some big dick energy right there.

I'd like to come visit you. I have a few requests if that's okay with you. I'll have my people forward you what I like to do when I travel without my wife. You know how us men are. Have lots of towels ready. (wink)

Glasnost,

Dollhands T. Rump

Dear Wives (past and present),

Hello ladies. My lawyer has asked that I write to you. It appears selling my soul may have been my best business deal yet! My wish to become President may come true.

The lawyers are worried an even bigger spotlight may shine upon you all, and they wanted me to remind you all that you've signed non-disclosure agreements concerning our relationships, divorces, affairs, my penis, etc. If we see anything in the tabloids or on the fake news channels, not only will your allowances be terminated, but you will be sued for everything you own.

Most importantly, since I'm trying to get the votes from all those evangelicals, they'd like us not to talk about how I cheated on my first wife with the woman who became my second wife. Or how I cheated on my second wife with a Playboy Playmate or how I cheated on my current wife with a Porn star. Fake Christians hate that stuff.

I'm also appealing to the people who claim to be Patriotic, so let's keep the fake bone spurs and me calling troops idiots and things like that on the down-low. Just keep pretending like we all support our troops, I'll hug a few flags for the cameras, and it will all be okay. The fact that these same voters still vote for Republicans, even though they vote against anything that helps Veterans, shows it's all just bullshit for them anyway. I'm not worried.

Just remember, I was the best husband you ever had. Any wrongdoing was your fault, my penis is enormous, and I believe in **G**od, our Troops, and support the Police. These idiots will eat it up.

Your Favorite Husband,

Dollhands T. Rump

Dear Global Warming Fanatics,

I went outside yesterday and it was cold. Coldest it's ever been. It was so cold that one of my nipples may have broken off. That, right there, shows what bullshit Global Warming is. How could it be the coldest it's ever been since probably the Ice Age, and we're freezing our asses off, and you're all crying about the Earth warming up?

And don't give me that crap about how Winter is also an effect of Global Warming. We all know the words Winter and Warm don't go together. Idiots.

Global warming is as fake as the vaccine, Obama's birth certificate, heart disease and all those accusations against me by women who say I sexually assaulted them.

Ice caps are fine. Sea levels are fine. Polar bears are everywhere. Only idiots believe what 99% of scientists say when that one guy on YouTube says the exact opposite.

All science is fake!

Nature Genius,

Dollhands T. Rump

To My Kids,

My sweet, beautiful daughter...and the rest of you. So, it looks like maybe your amazing dad might become President soon. The polls say I'm losing to that woman who should be in jail. Still, my experts tell me that there are enough morons, racists, neo-Nazis, fake patriots, homophobes, misogynists, and evangelicals out there, that we might just pull this off.

So here's the thing. The commie, left press will probably start asking you questions about your childhood, how I was as a father, stuff like that. Just make sure you tell them you had the best childhood, were loved by whichever mom you had growing up, and that I was the best dad in the world. So the truth!

My beautiful daughter — nothing you say is wrong, and you're fantastic to watch as you make words, so I'm not worried about you.

The boy named after me — you're kind of a hot head and loud, but your heart is in the right place. Just say as little as possible, wear your flannel shirts (Daddy knows how tough those make you feel), and try real hard to find that sweet spot between needing just one more hit and one too many. If I see you on the television with your eyes all bloodshot and you're talking too fast, I will get pissed. Focus.

To my other daughter — most people don't even know you exist or care, so great job. Keep it up.

Other son — I'm going to need you to refuse all interviews. Please don't talk to anyone, and dear God, boy, comb your hair! I expect you to be as seen as your other sister, who isn't your best sister, but at least she knows the art of keeping a low profile.

Oh shit, and to my youngest boy (I keep forgetting you're mine, mainly because your mom keeps you away at your school for rich kids and I'm still not sure she's told you I'm your father).

You'll probably be moving into the White House with us during your summer break. I've heard it's a pretty shitty and run down place, but I'll have them make your room real nice, just like you have at school. You'll love it. All your friends will be jealous. Any sign of that Chelsea girl will be completely removed. Hopefully her mom will be in jail by then, too.

Okay, remember, if it isn't about how great I was as a father, then your mouths better not be moving.

Daddy loves most of you,

Dollhands T. Rump

To The Republicans Running Against Me,

Dear Losers, you and I both know I'm going to win. I know because I know how to get into the hearts and minds of your idiot base. You see, my entire life I've said what I wanted and did what I wanted, which reminds people of how things used to be. When we kept women at home, the minorities knew their place, and everything was nice and white and wonderful.

As politicians, you've had to pretend you don't want that too. You've spent your whole life kissing ass and negotiating. That's why you will lose.

I'm not a politician. I'm a businessman, and a reality tv star, who has never had to answer to anyone but myself. If I don't like you, I say it. If you don't belong in America, guess what? You're gone! That is how we make America great again!

Now you all want to pretend like you hate how I act, but you're just jealous because I figured out something you haven't. Your voters are idiots.

They scream about being patriots, but when I saw them all attack John Kerry and his time in Vietnam, I knew I was safe making fun of a **POW** on tv. They scream they're for family values, but when I saw how they overlook all the Republicans accused of sex crimes, I knew my divorces and affairs wouldn't matter to them. They claim to want smaller government and lower taxes, but every Republican President has grown the government's size and left office with a larger deficit than when they came in. The **ONLY** time the debt has come down was under Democrat Presidents, but we need to keep calling them socialists, and Republican voters are happy to overlook that.

What you idiots have never figured out is the Republican Party **IS** the Party of Opposites. Over 100 bills to help veterans have been struck down by Republicans over the last two years. Evangelicals, my bread and butter, are so focused on abortion and gay marriage, two things **NOT** listed in the Ten Commandments, they're willing to overlook cheating and murder, two things that are. Throw some treason in there, and they don't mind. Suckers.

The fact that I'm a rich guy from New York, who was given money from his dad to make more money, has been sued over four thousand times, and has run almost every business I've owned into the ground doesn't even phase these idiots. They still call me a successful businessman because I told them I was. Sheep.

ALL they care about is one thing. Do I hate who they hate? Do I denounce atheists, progressives, overly-educated morons, science nerds, minorities, Muslims, women who don't know their place, loud Black people, Asians with their viruses, people from way far away who want to spread AIDS everywhere, Oprah, Socialists, Communists, Gays, Nancy Pelosi and Drag Queens? I do. And they love me for it.

You see, I hate who they hate. I make them believe I will fight to ensure no one drinks from their metaphorical water fountains. Fear and anger are what motivate them. That's what I offer. Win/win.

The Leader of the Party,

Dollhands T. Rump

Dear Jerks Who Call Me Racist,

First, let me start by saying I'm the least racist person you'll ever meet. Sure, in 1973, the Federal Government found me guilty of housing discrimination against Blacks, and in 1980, they revealed that whenever my wife and I would visit our casino, they would hide all the black employees. Or in 1989, when I demanded they kill the Central Park Five, even though they later said they were innocent (I don't believe it). All lies!

Just like in 1991, when I said that I don't like Black people counting my money and made a remark about how 'laziness is a trait in blacks... it's not anything they can control.' Or in 1992, when I was caught taking Black employees off the casino floor when one of my friends didn't like seeing them there. Or in 1993, when I fought against Indian casinos because I didn't think those Indians looked like Indians (they didn't), and then I said we know they're all criminals (they are). Or in 2005, when I suggested my TV show do a season that was White People vs. Black People (I still think that would be great!). Or in 2011, when I told David Letterman I was against building a mosque near Ground Zero because we all knew the Muslims were blowing us up. Or when I accused Barack HUSSAIN Obama of not being born in the United States (Where's the birth certificate)?

Then, just because I said that all Mexican immigrants were rapists and drug mules, and I tried to ban all Muslims from entering the U.S., and I said all 1.6 billion of them hated us, I didn't mean anything by that. It was just facts. Facts aren't racist.

It was all as unfair as when people got mad that I retweeted things from White Supremacists and said neo-Nazis were very fine people or called Senator Warren 'Pocahontas'. All innocent!

Then, when they uncovered that I wanted our military to shoot the Black Lives Matter protestors. It was a lie to say I wanted that because they were Black. I would have wanted them shot if they were Mexicans or Jews, or Asians as well. Oh, and speaking of Asians, all the false accusations that I was a racist just because I referred to the Covid virus as the China Flu, or the Chinese Virus, or the Kung Flu. Completely innocent and pretty scientifically accurate. All the best scientists agreed with me. The smart one, anyway.

These examples were all taken out of context and are just attacks by those who feel guilty about their own racism. I love the Blacks. My family has worked with, hired, owned, or slept with Blacks for years. Would a racist person do that?

Most of my staff is Black. My chef, driver, and the guy that lays out my suits and irons my giant, red ties are all Black. Except for the woman that makes up my bed, the Blacks are a big part of what keeps the Rump Empire running. Why aren't Blacks making up my bed? It's not because they're Black. It's hard to explain, but no one can make a bed like a little Mexican woman. It must be something they're born with.

The least racist person in America,

Dollhands T. Rump

Dear Golf Digest,

Now that it looks like I may be the President of **EVERYTHING** let's stop pretending I'm not the best golfer in the world. It's sad how you always pander to people like Obama and Tiger Woods when a talent like mine is out there, being ignored because of some golfing affirmative action bullshit. Sure, it's impressive that Black people can swing a club, swim, or have learned to play hockey, but that's no reason to fawn all over them. I'm a white guy that can rap. You don't see me getting all the hip-hop awards, do you?

Anyway, now that I am in charge, I give you full permission to tell the world what a fantastic golfer I am. It's not just about our scores on the Green. It's also about how we swing the club, who owns the course, what the caddy is willing to do to stay in our good graces, how much money we contribute to your magazine, where we plan on burying our wives (that would be the near the 18th hole) and so many other things that, when looked at properly, make a great golfer.

Some of the greatest golfers have told me, 'Mr. Future President, if only we could play golf like you'. It's all true. I would never lie about that. One golfer, I won't name names, but his name rhymes with **Gill Gicholson**, he told me that I had the whitest balls he's ever seen. **Come** to think of it, those Russian ladies told me the same thing, which is weird, because we weren't even playing golf.

Anyway, I'm ready for your article about how I'm a better golfer than Obama and Tiger, and let me know when you want me to come in to do the photo shoot for the cover of your magazine. I'll wear my sexy white golf shorts. The ladies love them. We can call me The President of Golf! The article can be called Making Golf Great Again! A trophy would be nice too. And one of those jackets, but not that stupid green color, I need something that goes with my red tie and my beautiful tan. I'm excited!

Oh, and did I tell you I'm helping to repeal those laws that say everyone has to be allowed to join a golf club? It's true. I'm not saying certain people won't be allowed in the club because we need someone to water the grass and make our lunches, but we should have the freedom to decide what type of people we have to see out on the greens with us. It would be Socialism to tell the wealthiest people they can't only surround themselves with the people they want. That's called FREEDOM! This is America.

My people will be contacting your people,

President (soon) Dollhands T. Rump

Oval Office

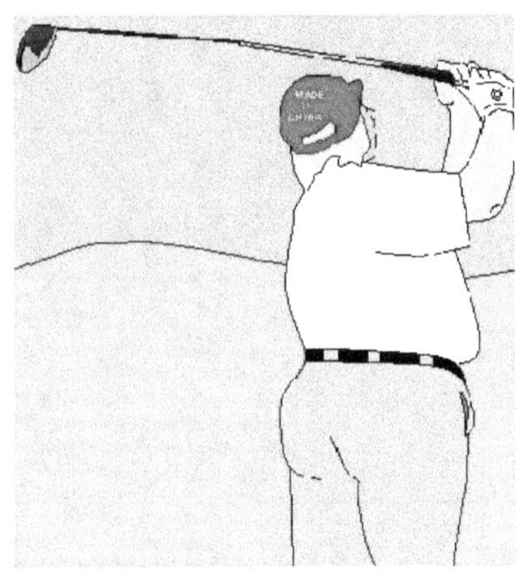
MADE
IN
CHINA

Dear America,

It looks like you have made me your President. At least the dumb ones did. This is going to be fun.

I will hug flags, terrorize brown people, piss off the gays, call everyone a socialist, and make you morons donate money to me while you eventually commit treason toward your own country...and you'll thank me for it!

Now get some Vaseline and bend over

...time to Make America Great Again!

Your President and Cult Leader,

Dollhands T. Rump

That's the end of the book.

If you bought it because you think the orange guy is an idiot...he's still an idiot. Sorry.

If you bought it because you thought you were getting something about the moron that was complimentary, you're even dumber than we thought. Sad.

Go do something